Christmas is About JESUS

An Advent Devotional

TATE PUBLISHING
& *Enterprises*

Blessings,
Mukkove

by Mukkove Johnson

Dedicated to

Maciah, Wyatt, and Karissa.

May you come to know *everything* is about Jesus.

Published by Tate Publishing & Enterprises, LLC
127 E. Trade Center Terrace | Mustang, Oklahoma 73064 USA
1.888.361.9473 | www.tatepublishing.com

Tate Publishing is committed to excellence in the publishing industry. The company reflects the philosophy established by the founders, based on Psalm 68:11,
"The Lord gave the word and great was the company of those who published it."

Cover and Interior design by Eddie Russell
Illustration by Jason Hutton

Published in the United States of America

ISBN: 978-1-60799-712-2
1. Juvenile Nonfiction: Holidays & Celebrations: Christmas & Advent
2. Juvenile Nonfiction: Religion: Bible Stories: New Testament
09.06.29

A Note from the Author

Dear Parent,

Christmas is a wonderfully busy time. Keeping our children's focus on the real purpose of Christmas can be quite challenging. Like you, I wanted my children to remember why we celebrate Christmas. I never wanted them to think it was all about getting presents or Santa Claus. Out of those desires this book was born. Our family has enjoyed this Advent tradition for several years. Now I have the opportunity to share it with your family. Starting on December 1, each day has a devotion of how a symbol of Christmas reminds us of Jesus. Each devotion has a saying and a verse. Christmas Day does not have a devotion. Our family enjoys reading the Christmas story from the Bible Christmas morning.

As you go through your preparations and celebrations, you can talk about the things you see that you have read about in *Christmas Is about Jesus.* Reading the daily story will have far greater impact if, as commanded in Deuteronomy 6:7, you "impress them on your children. Talk about them when you sit at home and when you walk [or drive] along the road, when you lie down and when you get up." (NIV) I hope your family will enjoy and be blessed this and every Christmas season.

Blessings in Jesus,
Mukkove Johnson

December 1st

Snowflakes

Jesus Made Me Special

I praise you because you made me in an amazing and wonderful way. What you have done is wonderful. I know this very well.

Psalm 139:14

Snowflakes are so beautiful. There are no two snowflakes exactly alike. Can you imagine God taking time to make each snowflake different? God makes every person special and different, too. Do you know you are different from every other person that has ever been born? Wow!

God designed you just the way you are. God gave you just the right hair and eyes, nose and toes. God gave you your laugh and your smile. Jesus knows your name and even how many hairs are on your head! He loves you very much. Jesus is one of a kind in a different way. He is the only Son of God, the only person ever to be all man and all God. That's why Jesus is the only one who can be the Savior and forgive your sins. Can you thank God for making you special and unique like a snowflake? Will you thank him for Jesus, too?

December 2nd

Snow

Jesus Makes us Clean

The Lord says, "Come, we will talk theses things over. Your sins are red like deep cloth. But they can be as white as snow."

Isaiah 1:18a

Do you get to go out and play in the snow at Christmas time? The snow covers the ground and makes everything look new and clean. The whole world looks beautiful, pure, and white.

Snow can remind you of Jesus. He is beautiful, clean, and pure. Jesus lived his life and never did anything wrong. When Jesus died, he didn't stay dead. Jesus is alive. Do you believe in Jesus? Then you can be forgiven of all the things you have done wrong. When you tell God what you have done wrong, he will forgive you. You can be made pure and clean like Jesus. Do you know what that means? Jesus will be your friend now, and you will live with God in heaven after you die.

December 3rd

Ornaments

Show People Jesus

Jesus said, "Go home to your family and friends. Tell them how much the Lord has done for you and how He has had mercy on you."

Mark 5:19b

Ornaments are beautiful. They are shiny and bright. You can see them decorating trees and windows. Do the ornaments on your tree have special stories and memories? Have you made some of the ornaments on your tree? Ornaments are for everyone to enjoy. They can help you to remember past Christmases and that Christmas is about Jesus.

When Jesus was on earth people enjoyed being around him. People should like to be around you, too. You can be kind and loving toward people. You can love people with God's love, just like Jesus did. Maybe you will have a chance to tell them about the love of Jesus if you show it to them first. How can you live in a way that will show people Jesus?

December 4th

Candy Cane

Jesus is The Rock

"Everyone who hears these things I say and obeys them is like a wise man. The wise man built his house on rock."

Luke 7:24

Have you heard candy canes were made just to tell people about Jesus? Candy is sweet, like the Good News that God loves you and has great plans for you. The white reminds you of Jesus's holiness. The red stripes remind you of Jesus's blood. The peppermint flavor is similar to a flavor the Bible calls hyssop, which means "to make something clean." Jesus makes you clean from your sins when you ask him. The shape of the candy cane one way is a "J" for Jesus; the other way it's a shepherd's staff, because Jesus is The Good Shepherd. The hardness of the candy cane reminds you Jesus is your "Rock," very steady, a good place to build your life. Jesus never changes his mind or his promises. Do you trust Jesus to be the firm foundation for your life?

December 5th

St. Nicholas

Serve Jesus by Giving

Remember this: The person who plants a little will have a small harvest. But the person who plants a lot will have a big harvest. Each one should give, then, what he has decided in his heart to give. He should not give if it makes him sad. And he should not give if he thinks he is forced to give. God loves the person who gives happily.

2 Corinthians 9:6, 7

Everywhere you look at Christmas time you see Santa Claus or St. Nicholas. Did you ever wonder why? The real Santa Claus, St. Nicholas, was born in Turkey long ago. He loved God very much, even as a boy. He loved to give gifts. The government did not like Christians and Nicholas was put in prison for being a Christian.

Nicholas is remembered for his love of children and his giving. He saved people from slavery and hunger. People that knew about him thought he was good enough to be made a saint in the Catholic Church. So he became St. Nicholas. His name and the traditions surrounding him are different all over the world. The important thing to remember is that Nicholas loved Jesus and shared Jesus's love with others by giving his money and his time. Is there any way you and your family can give to God by helping people in need this Christmas?

December 6th

Hats

Jesus is King of Kings

On his robe and on his leg was written this name "King of Kings and Lord of Lords."

Revelation 19:16

What kinds of hats do you see at Christmas? Some people wear hats because it is cold outside. Some wear Santa Claus hats. Some hats tell you about what people do. Police and soldiers wear hats as part of their uniform; so do firefighters. Jesus only wore one special kind of hat on his head when he was on earth. It was a crown of thorns. Jesus didn't want to wear the crown of thorns; mean people pushed it onto his head before he died for your sins.

Jesus is the King of Kings. The crown he wears now is more beautiful than can be imagined. Do you know the Bible says that one day, if you believe and serve Jesus, you will receive crowns, too? When you see all the Santa Claus hats, you can think of the crown King Jesus wears and the one he will give to you one day.

December 7th

Christmas Trees

Jesus is The Life

Jesus said to her, "I am the resurrection and the life. He who believes in me will have life even if he dies."

John 11:25

Does your family decorate a Christmas tree? Christmas trees remind you of Jesus in many ways. Christmas trees are green showing they are alive. Jesus came to give you life. Christmas trees are always green. Even through trials and hard times like winter, they stay green. Jesus is still alive. He gives you life now and forever if you believe. Trees point up, where Jesus went after he finished his work on earth. The cross Jesus died on was made from a tree. Trees provide shelter and protection. Jesus provides salvation, life, and other needs for each one who follows him. Will you remember Jesus when you see all the beautiful trees at Christmas?

December 8th

Christmas Lights

Jesus is the Light

Later Jesus talked to the people again. He said, "I am the Light of the world. The person who follows me will never live in darkness. He will have the light that gives life."

John 8:12

People put lights everywhere at Christmas. You see them on houses and trees. Some people even have lights on their jewelry or neckties! Why all the lights? To say Jesus is the Light of the World.

Light is like Jesus in many ways. Light is very special because you cannot make it dirty. Jesus came to the world and lived around people who did things wrong, but he never did anything wrong. Light can always be seen no matter how dark it is. Jesus is always with you no matter where you are, what you've done, or what's happened to you. Jesus shines his light of hope like a flashlight in the dark. Without Jesus, you can never be good enough for God to let you into heaven or to have a relationship with him. That is a very dark, hopeless thought. Jesus came to be the way for you to go to heaven. Jesus came to make you God's friend. That is a very light, hopeful thought. How can you tell someone Jesus is the Light?

December 9th

Fruit

Jesus is the Vine

"I am the vine, and you are the branches. If a person remains in me and I remain in him, then he produces much fruit. But without me he can do nothing."

John 15:5

Grapes grow on vines. If a branch is cut off the vine, it will not grow any grapes. In fact it will die. Jesus called himself the "vine" and said believers in him are branches. Like the grapevine gives life to the branches, Jesus gives life to you. When you believe in Jesus, you should grow to be more like him.

You will begin to grow the Fruit of the Spirit in your life "love, joy, peace, patience, kindness, goodness, faithfulness, gentleness, self-control." (Galatians 5:22, 23a, NIV) You can not grow this fruit on your own. You need help from Jesus. How do you stay connected to Jesus? Are you letting Jesus grow good fruit through you?

December 10th

Cookies

Jesus is the Bread of Life

Then Jesus said, "I am the bread that gives life. He who comes to me will never be hungry. He who believes in me will never be thirsty."

John 6:35

Do you like to eat cookies? Cookies are just one of many special foods people enjoy at Christmas. What are some special foods your family enjoys? Special foods at Christmas are just extra and fun. You don't need them to survive. Do you know you need spiritual food?

Jesus said he was the Bread of Life. You need Jesus every day just like you need food every day. Even with all the special foods, you will get hungry again. Jesus tells you to feed on his Word, the Bible, and you will never be hungry again. Of course you still have to eat. Jesus is talking about spiritual hunger. If you are spiritually hungry, Jesus is the Bread who can satisfy. How can you eat the Bread of Life?

December 11th

Doves

Jesus is the Prince of Peace

A Child will be born to us. God will give a son to us. He will be responsible for leading the people. His name will be called Wonderful Counselor, Powerful God, Father Who Lives Forever, Prince of Peace.

Isaiah 9:6

Have you seen doves in Christmas decorations? Doves stand for peace. Jesus is called the Prince of Peace. The angel told the shepherds the Savior had come to bring peace to people. The peace that Jesus brings does not mean there won't be any more wars or fighting. Jesus brings peace you can have on the inside no matter what is going on outside: peace knowing God loves you, peace knowing God has forgiven all your sins and will take you to heaven one day, peace knowing God will never leave you and will always take care of you, peace knowing God is working all things out for your good. Will you make Jesus your Prince of Peace?

December 12th

Bells

Jesus is Coming Again

"You saw Jesus taken away from you into heaven. He will come back in the same way you saw him go."

Acts 1:11b

Bells are shiny and bright. They are beautiful and make wonderful music. You can enjoy seeing and hearing them, especially at Christmas. Bells were used to let people know what was happening. The bells would ring for the time of day and for church service. Bells would announce celebrations like weddings and toll slowly when announcing someone had died.

Like the bells making announcements, God gave his people many announcements about a Messiah. These promises are written in the Old Testament. The promises told where the Messiah would be born, who his family would be, the life the Messiah would live, and how he would die and come back to life again. There are also many promises about Jesus coming again to set up his eternal kingdom. You know Jesus will come again, because all the promises God made about sending a Messiah came true the first Christmas. When you see bells, ask, "Am I ready for Jesus to come again?"

December 13th

Songs

Worship Jesus

And Mary said: "My soul praises the Lord, and my heart is happy because God is my Savior."

Luke 1:46, 47

Songs have been part of Christmas since the very first. Mary sang about being the mother of Jesus. The angels sang praises to God after telling the good news of Jesus birth. There are many songs that are fun to sing. Many more songs tell the amazing story of that first Christmas when God became a man. Listen closely to the songs this Christmas. Who's telling the story? Sometimes it's Mary, sometimes the shepherds. Could it sometimes be you telling the story of Christmas being about Jesus? Will you sing songs this Christmas that worship Jesus?

December 14th

Candles

Share Jesus' Light

"In the same way, you should be a light for other people. Live so they will see the good things you do. Live so that they will praise your Father in heaven."

Matthew 5:16

Candles used to be the only light people had after the sun went down. The candles had to be set up high to spread their light as far as possible. Now candles are mostly used for decoration. As some families celebrate Advent, they light a candle each week for the four weeks before Christmas Day.

Candles can remind you Jesus wants you to be a light to the people around you. You can be a light by being loving and kind, like Jesus. When you act like Jesus, you show people Jesus loves them. You spread the light of Jesus by telling others what Jesus has done for you. Jesus forgives your sins. He will forgive the sins of anyone who asks him. He is with you all the time. How will you share Jesus's light?

December 15th

Holly

Jesus Suffered for Me

That is what you were called to do. Christ suffered for you. He gave you an example to follow. So you should do as he did.

1 Peter 2:21

Long ago people used holly plants to decorate their homes at Christmas. The green plants brought life into the homes during the dark winter. Holly reminds you Jesus came to give you life. The leaves of the holly have sharp points like the crown of thorns Jesus had to wear. The holly blossom is white, to remind you of Jesus's purity. The blossom turns to a red berry. Red is for the blood Jesus shed for everyone's sins. Holly also has a bitter tasting bark. Jesus faced many bitter things when he lived on earth. When you see holly, remember Jesus loved you enough to suffer for you. Have you thanked Jesus for loving you so much?

This is how God showed his love to us: He sent his only Son into the world to give us life through him.

1 John 4:9

December 16th

Gifts

Jesus is the Best Gift

The first Christmas gift was from God to every person on earth. He sent his very own Son to be the Savior for each person who would receive his gift. The next gifts were brought to Jesus by the wise men. Today people give gifts to people they love and care about and to people who do not have things they need. If you give a toy to a child who doesn't have any, you are giving it to God.

You can give the gift that God gave the first Christmas by telling people about Jesus. Can you think of a way to include the best gift, Jesus, with your other gifts?

December 17th

Wise Men

Obey Jesus

"If you love me, you will do the things I command."

John 14:15

The wise men in the Christmas story lived very far away from where Jesus was born. They loved to study the stars. When they were studying the stars, they noticed a special star. It was so special they decided it meant a great king had been born. They knew they had to make a long journey to see this king and worship him. The wise men found Jesus and his family in Bethlehem and gave them gifts for a king.

The Wise men put a lot of effort and time into finding Jesus so they could honor him. They gave him their best gifts. Jesus gave his very best for you. Will you give him your very best?

December 18th

Stars

Jesus is the Way

Jesus answered, "I am the way. And I am the truth and the life. The only way to the Father is through me."

John 14:6

There was a very special star on the first Christmas. Scholars from far away countries noticed the special star. The star told them someone special had been born. The star showed the way for the wise men to find Jesus. They found the King who had been born and worshiped him.

Jesus gives you many things to show you the way to live. He gives you parents and other adults to teach you right from wrong. The Bible tells you things God wants you to know about God and the way to live. Jesus showed you to live loving people with God's love. Creation shows you how awesome God is. Stars are part of God's creation. Even today they tell people about Jesus, the creator. Can you tell people Jesus is the Way?

December 19th

Sheep

Jesus is the Lamb of God

He saw Jesus walking by and said, "Look, the Lamb of God!"

John 1:36

At the time Jesus was born, God's people made sacrifices of animals to show God they were sorry for the things they had done wrong. One of the animals they used was a lamb. The lamb had to be perfect, but really even the perfect lambs could not take away people's sins. The people were obeying God by giving the sacrifices, and that was very important.

Jesus came to be the final sacrifice to take care of everyone's sin. Jesus lived life making no mistakes; he was perfect. His death was the perfect sacrifice. You have to believe God did this for you. There is no need to make sacrifices of animals anymore. Do you believe God is satisfied? Jesus is the perfect Lamb of God who takes away the sin of the world and all of your sins, too.

When they had seen him, they spread the word concerning what had been told them about this child.

Luke 2:17 (NIV)

December 20th

Shepherds

Shepherds Share the Good News

Shepherds were outside watching their sheep near Bethlehem on the night Jesus was born. Things were going along as usual when an angel appeared. The shepherds were very afraid. Would you have been afraid? The angel told them not to be afraid. He had good news. The Messiah they were waiting for had been born. Suddenly, the whole sky was filled with angels singing praises to God.

The shepherds went right away to find the baby. After they saw Jesus, they told Mary what they had seen. The shepherds went and told everyone they could about the wonderful things that had happened. Shepherds remind us to share with others that Christmas is about Jesus. Can you be like the shepherds and tell what God has done for you?

December 21st

Shepherd

Jesus is The Good Shepherd

"I am the good shepherd. The good shepherd gives his life for the sheep... My sheep listen to my voice. I know them, and they follow me."

John 10:11 & 27

Sheep do not worry about what they will eat. They do not worry if they will have water to drink. They do not think about where they will sleep. They just follow their shepherd's voice, because they know he will take care of them.

Jesus is the Good Shepherd. He makes sure you have people to take care of you, have food to eat, and a place to sleep. Jesus gives you strength and wisdom to make good choices. God sends the Holy Spirit to be with you, to teach you and comfort you. If you believe in him, Jesus makes sure you have a place to live forever in heaven. Do you know Jesus's voice and follow him?

December 22nd

Angels

Angels Bring News of Jesus

The angel said to them, "Don't be afraid, because I am bringing you some good news. It will be a joy to all people."

Luke 2:10

Do you have an angel on the top of your Christmas tree? The angels were busy getting ready for that first Christmas. They first delivered a message telling Zechariah he would be the father of John the Baptist. Then the angel told Mary her good news. Then good news for Joseph. Joseph was going to help Mary raise Jesus to be a man of God.

The angels were most excited to tell the shepherds around Bethlehem that the Savior had been born. What exciting news! The angels filled the sky with light and song, praising God. Can you bring others the Good News of Jesus and give praise to God when you see angels this Christmas?

December 23st

Mary

Say Yes to Jesus

Mary said, "I am the servant girl of the Lord. Let this happen to me as you say!"

Luke 1:38

Mary loved God and pleased God by the way she lived. God chose her to be the mother of the Savior, Jesus. An angel came to tell her the news. She was afraid and confused. The angel told her everything would be okay. Mary said, "Yes, I will do what God wants me to do." She sang a song to thank God for choosing her to serve him in such a special way. Can you sing a song to God, too? Will you say "Yes" to the plans God has for your life?

December 24th

Jesus

Christmas is About Jesus

Today your Savior was born in David's town. He is Christ, the Lord.

Luke 2:11

Jesus came to earth many, many years ago. His birth was very special. Jesus was God, but he was born a baby just like you. Christmas is the time of year when you celebrate Jesus birthday. That's why Christmas is about Jesus. Sure there are gifts, decorations, food, and fun, but Christmas is about Jesus.

Jesus became a man so you could be forgiven of the things you've done wrong. He loves you so very much. Jesus wants to be your friend. That's a great reason to celebrate! How will you celebrate Jesus?

e|LIVE

listen|imagine|view|experience

AUDIO BOOK DOWNLOAD INCLUDED WITH THIS BOOK!

In your hands you hold a complete digital entertainment package. Besides purchasing the paper version of this book, this book includes a free download of the audio version of this book. Simply use the code listed below when visiting our website. Once downloaded to your computer, you can listen to the book through your computer's speakers, burn it to an audio CD or save the file to your portable music device (such as Apple's popular iPod) and listen on the go!

How to get your free audio book digital download:

1. Visit www.tatepublishing.com and click on the e|LIVE logo on the home page.
2. Enter the following coupon code:
   3a02-af9e-1c3e-e02d-6738-4f45-5c29-7081
3. Download the audio book from your e|LIVE digital locker and begin enjoying your new digital entertainment package today!